WORDS OF POWER
VOICES FROM INDIAN AMERICA

◊◊◊◊◊

Edited by
Norbert S. Hill, Jr., Oneida

FULCRUM PUBLISHING
GOLDEN, COLORADO

Several quotations have been reprinted from the following sources:
Reprinted from *Sitting Bull: Champion of the Sioux*, by Stanley Vestal;
University of Oklahoma Press, 1005 Asp Ave., Norman, OK 73019
Reprinted from *Profiles in Wisdom*, by Steven McFadden, Copyright 1991,
Bear & Co. Inc., P.O. Box 2860, Santa Fe, NM 87504
Reprinted from *Indian Oratory*, by W.C. Vanderwerth;
University of Oklahoma Press, 1005 Asp Avenue, Norman, OK 73019
Reprinted from *Circle Without End*, by Frances G. and Gerald Scott Lombardi;
Naturegraph Publishers, Inc., P.O. Box 1075, Happy Camp, CA 96039

Book and cover design by Jane Hopkins
Cover image by Sam English copyright © 1994 Sam English

Library of Congress Cataloging-in-Publication Data

Words of power: voices from Indian America / edited by
Norbert S. Hill, Jr.
p.   cm.
ISBN 1-55591-189-7
1. Indian philosophy—north America. 2. Quotations,
American.
I. Hill, Norbert S.
E98.P5W67—dc20   94-27436
                                  CIP

Printed in the United States of America
0 9 8 7 6 5 4 3 2 1

Fulcrum Publishing
350 Indiana Street, Suite 350
Golden, Colorado 80401-5093
(800) 992-2908

American Indian Science and Engineering Society (AISES)
1630 30th Street, Suite 301
Boulder, Colorado 80301-1014
(303) 492-8658

CONTENTS

◊	FOREWORD	v
◊	INTRODUCTION	ix
One	VALUES	1
Two	SPIRITUALITY, RELIGION	5
Three	TRADITION, HISTORY	10
Four	WOMEN AND MEN	15
Five	CHILDREN, EDUCATION	19
Six	ECONOMICS, MONEY AND POWER	22
Seven	LAND, ENVIRONMENT	25
Eight	INSIGHT, APPRECIATION	31
Nine	PHILOSOPHY, CULTURE	35
Ten	LEADERSHIP	39
Eleven	STRUGGLE, CONFLICT, TREATIES	43
Twelve	JUSTICE, RECONCILIATION, PEACE	47
Thirteen	COMMUNITY	50
◊	SOURCES	53
◊	INDEX OF SPEAKERS	55

FOREWORD

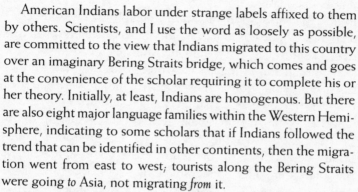

American Indians labor under strange labels affixed to them by others. Scientists, and I use the word as loosely as possible, are committed to the view that Indians migrated to this country over an imaginary Bering Straits bridge, which comes and goes at the convenience of the scholar requiring it to complete his or her theory. Initially, at least, Indians are homogenous. But there are also eight major language families within the Western Hemisphere, indicating to some scholars that if Indians followed the trend that can be identified in other continents, then the migration went from east to west; tourists along the Bering Straits were going *to* Asia, not migrating *from* it.

The reservation system was foisted upon all Indian nations regardless of the nation's condition, and in the eyes of the federal policy makers, 160 acres per tribal member was adequate to make a living—whether it was a tract of lush grasslands or a desert filled with cactus and creosote. Until the New Deal and John Collier's support for traditional ways, Indian tribes were seen as homogenous in everything except language. In our immediate past, it has become popular to stress the dissimilarities of the Indian nations, and sometimes these distinctions become barriers to the creation and administration of national policy.

This background of conceptual oppression and confusion is necessary because two great truths exist side by side: (1) Indian nations are quite distinct from each other and (2) there is a great unanimity among Indian peoples when they express their views on the natural world and on the behavior of humans in that world.

Often, unless an individual is specifically identified as being of a particular Indian nation, his or her sentiments about the world cannot be distinguished by tribal particularity. It is, therefore, entirely possible to talk of an "Indian" philosophy that has so many common characteristics that it can be said to link the various Indian nations metaphysically and yet to recognize that each Indian nation has particular knowledge that is sophisticated and uniquely site-specific.

For decades, non-Indians have produced coffee table books filled with sepia photographs of elderly Indians with captions that describe, in poetic fashion, some insight into the natural world and human experiences within it. The glaring omission of these books is the paucity of quotations from contemporary people. Indeed, the tenor of the books is to suggest that there were once poetic, romantic people roaming North America who spoke in clever aphorisms and understood everything about life that was worth knowing. Modern Indians then, hastily escorted to a few quotations at the end of these volumes, were regarded as mere remnants of a once-great people who mysteriously disappeared sometime around 1890.

This book of quotations is meant to be different. Deliberate care has been exercised to produce a mixture of older and modern Indian sayings, demonstrating that while peoples and conditions may change, in fact the basic perspective of Indian people remains remarkably constant. A close reading of the sayings in this book will validate this contention. Indeed, aside from the fact that people are addressing the concerns of their generation and, consequently, phrasing their comments to the subject at hand, there is virtually *no difference in outlook whatsoever*.

The American Indian Science and Engineering Society has been organizing conferences on the traditional knowledge of the natural world, although in Indian understandings there is nothing *but* a natural world. The outstanding aspect of this knowledge, as it has been transmitted to the participants, is that all information about the world we live in has a moral content and is directed at the relationships that humans enjoy with the world and its creatures. It is the moral dimension that makes knowledge whole and useful and requires the individual to act in a manner consistent with his or her beliefs and understanding of things.

Western civilization, unfortunately, does not link knowledge and morality but rather, it connects knowledge and power and makes them equivalent. Today with an information "superhighway" now looming on the horizon, we are told that a lack of access to information will doom people to a life of meaninglessness—and poverty. As we look around and observe modern industrial society, however, there is no question that information, in and of itself, is useless and that as more data is generated, ethical and moral decisions are taking on a fantasy dimension in which a "lack of evidence to indict" is the moral equivalent of the good deed.

This volume, therefore, is a dangerous piece of information if the readers take it seriously. Its selections speak of a time and a cultural context in which consistency and integrity were the struts and buttresses of human society. Today, even in many Indian nations, these sets of moral responsibilities have come loose, and leadership is defined as taking more than one's share as quickly as possible. Too often today words are mistaken for deeds so that expressing a fine sentiment is the equivalent of acting in a moral way.

Indian people in particular must take these quotations to heart and dwell on their inner meanings and not simply enjoy the poetic crafting of ideas. A major flaw in Indian country today is that the large number of educated Indians, lawyers, teachers, economic developers, organizational executives have been filled with information but know not the meaning or moral connections that this data should have in order to be useful to their people. Indian politicians frequently quote Black Elk, Standing Bear and other great sages, but they seem to miss the demand that doing and not talking is required.

There is a popular saying in Indian country that each generation must provide for the seven generations that follow it. Within this book we have the collected wisdom of many tribes, many individuals and many generations. We stand under the judgment of the generations that went before us and whom we shall meet when our generation passes on. The similarity in perspective that is demonstrated in these collected quotations shows that the teachings of past generations have been handed down with the same vibrant moral content that guided our ancestors. It is up to this generation to put these ideas once more into the active lives of our people and to bring them full circle to the social reality of Indian Life.

—Vine Deloria, Jr.

INTRODUCTION

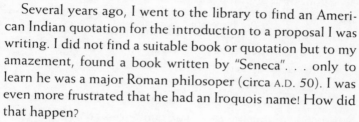

Several years ago, I went to the library to find an American Indian quotation for the introduction to a proposal I was writing. I did not find a suitable book or quotation but to my amazement, found a book written by "Seneca". . . only to learn he was a major Roman philosoper (circa A.D. 50). I was even more frustrated that he had an Iroquois name! How did that happen?

The need for a book of American Indian quotations has stuck in my mind since then. There should be many on the library shelves of America. I am reminded of a line from a poem my father wrote: "Speak Softly, Walk Humbly, And Act Compassionately." All of the quotations in this small volume embody these qualities.

We struggle to find our own voices and our own story. They are all around us—in the past, the present and the future. Some of the voices are born of oppression, ceremony, fear or celebration—linking the old and the new, the visible and the invisible. There is a continuum: thoughts, memory, words, songs, prayers and spirit. In this blending of Indian voices there is power in the collective; bundled together they are even more powerful, more profound.

American Indian ways are different, not wrong. Our contemporary expressions and knowledge are built on the shoulders of our history. This is a book of Indian voices from the past as well as today; it is naturally only a small fraction of the wisdom, either current or past, and a quotation can only lead the reader in the direction of a larger, deeper body of knowledge. Quotations are simultaneously simple and sacred. This is a book for quiet reflection, not action. American Indians share a hunger for memory; this is a book of memory.

Sometimes we tend to romanticize the past as an ideal state, long gone and forgotten. But our ancestors struggled and loved then as we do today. We live, as they did, in a world of contradictions and paradoxes. But the storyteller lives forever and bridges the past and present in our minds and in our hearts. Quotations are merely the sound bites of a story—a glimmer of a larger context.

This book is composed of enduring bits of wisdom that transcend culture and race. The quotations are gifts to future generations, humbly passed through us to you. This is only a small portion of what is available, a fraction of what has been lost, perhaps small in comparison to what may yet be said. We hope it will be the beginning of a journey for our readers.

—Norbert S. Hill, Jr. (Oneida)

You have noticed that everything an Indian does is in a circle, and that is because the Power of the World always works in circles, and everything tries to be round. ... Everything the Power of the World does is done in a circle. The sky is round ... and so are all the stars. The wind, in its greatest power whirls. Birds make their nests in circles, for theirs is the same religion as ours. The sun comes forth and goes down again in a circle. The moon does the same, and both are round. Even the seasons form a great circle in their changing, and always come back again to where they were. The life of a man is a circle from childhood to childhood and so it is in everything where power moves.

BLACK ELK, OGLALA LAKOTA, 1930

VALUES

From the time the Indian first set foot upon this continent, he centered his life in the natural world. He is deeply invested in the earth, committed to it both in his consciousness and in his instinct. To him the sense of place is paramount. Only in reference to the earth can he persist in his true identity.

N. SCOTT MOMADAY, KIOWA, 1974

The transference or transmutation of values lies at the heart of problems in Indian country. And Indian country is an affectionate term for the whole earth—the land, mother earth, father sky, the four grandfather winds, the grandmother moon and her seeds that give us life. To forget or ignore basic Indian values, traditional values, human values, natural law—is a crime.

KARONIAKTATIE (ALEX JACOBS), MOHAWK, 1989

There is nothing in natural life, in Indian life, that fears death. It is natural. It is a part of life. We know that, but we've been taught fear. I have never had any difficulty reconciling the teachings of Christ, or any other great teacher as I understand them, with what I hear and what I feel. The one missing element that I do understand, something of Indianness that sometimes in our polite society we leave out, is the realization that we cannot live until we are ready to die. We must realize that we all pass through. You cannot have the fear of death in front of you and have a full life.

GENE KELUCHE, WINTU, 1992

Touch not the poisonous firewater that makes wise men turn to fools and robs the spirit of its vision.

TECUMSEH, SHAWNEE, C. 1800

No one likes to be criticized, but criticism can be something like the desert wind that, in whipping the tender stalks, forces them to strike their roots down deeper for security.

POLINGAYSI QÖYAWAYMA, HOPI, 1964

2

Love is something that you can leave behind you when you die. It's that powerful.

JOHN (FIRE) LAME DEER, ROSEBUD LAKOTA, 1972

Don't be afraid to cry. It will free your mind of sorrowful thoughts.

DON TALAYESVA, HOPI, C. 1940

The elders remind us of the importance of the long view when they say, "pin peyeh obe"—look to the mountain. They use this phrase to remind us that we need to look at things as if we are looking out from the top of a mountain, seeing things in the much broader perspective of the generations that are yet to come. They remind us that in dealing with the landscape we must think in terms of a ten-thousand, twenty-thousand, or thirty-thousand-year relationship.

DR. GREGORY CAJETE, TEWA, 1993

Laughter—that is something very sacred, especially for us Indians.

JOHN (FIRE) LAME DEER, ROSEBUD LAKOTA, C. 1972

If you can develop an adequate self-image, then you are capable of directing your life, of making your own decision to turn against materialism. You have to have confidence in your own ability to be able to go it alone, to go against what the rest of the culture is doing.

DR. EUNICE BAUMANN-NELSON, PENOBSCOT, 1991

We love quiet; we suffer the mouse to play; when the woods are rustled by the wind, we fear not.

INDIAN CHIEF TO THE GOVERNOR OF PENNSYLVANIA, 1796

I appeal to any white man to say if he ever entered Logan's cabin hungry and he gave him not meat; if he ever came cold and naked and he clothed him not. During the course of the last long and bloody war, Logan remained idle in his cabin, an advocate for peace. Such was my love for the whites that my countrymen pointed as I passed and said, "Logan is a friend of the white man."

TACHNECHDORUS (LOGAN), MINGO CHIEF, 1774

I know that our people possessed remarkable powers of concentration and abstraction, and I sometimes fancy that such nearness to nature as I have described keeps the spirit sensitive to impressions not commonly felt, and in touch with the unseen powers.

OHIYESA (DR. CHARLES A. EASTMAN), SANTEE SIOUX, 1911

It is a strict law that bids us dance. It is a strict law that bids us distribute our property among our friends and neighbors. It is a good law. Let the white man observe his law, we shall observe ours.

ANONYMOUS, KWAKIUTL, 1886

Search for the truth. Indian values teach the holistic approach to the use of technology for mankind's good.

AL QÖYAWAYMA, HOPI, 1984

Hills are always more beautiful than stone buildings, you know. Living in a city is an artificial existence. Lots of people hardly ever feel real soil under their feet, see plants grow except in flower pots, or get far enough beyond the street light to catch the enchantment of a night sky studded with stars. When people live far from scenes of the Great Spirit's making, it's easy for them to forget his laws.

TATANGA MANI (WALKING BUFFALO), STONEY, 1958

◊ ◊ ◊ ◊ ◊

SPIRITUALITY, RELIGION

It is about respect—respect for everybody. In our understanding, the Creator made everything. That's all we're told.
He made everything. And since he made everything, then
you must respect everything. That's simple. And so as I look
upon you, I know that the Creator made you; I know that
you're equal. You're equal in every way to us. And I respect
you because you are a manifestation of the Creation.

But, the law says that you must respect us as well. In this
basic respect is peace. That's what's called community. Unfortunately, in today's time this does not occur. And so what
I am talking about now is respect for our people's ways. Our

land, our language, and our culture have been taken. Don't try to take our religion. We need that respect.

OREN LYONS, ONONDAGA, 1992

I think there was a big mistake made (when) people separated religion and the government. That was one of the big mistakes that was made, because when they did that, then they removed the Creator from their life—or at least from half to three-quarters of their life.

TOM PORTER, MOHAWK, 1991

The greatest obstacle to the internal nature is the mind. If it relies on logic such as the white man's mind, the domain of the inner nature is inaccessible. The simple fact is a man does not challenge the wisdom of the Holy Mystery.

TURTLEHEART, TETON SIOUX, 1967

Each soul must meet the morning sun, the new sweet earth and the Great Silence alone!

OHIYESA (DR. CHARLES A. EASTMAN), SANTEE SIOUX, 1911

We, the religious leaders and rightful spokesmen for the Hopi Independent Nation, have been instructed by the Great Spirit to express the invitation to the President of the United States and all spiritual leaders everywhere to meet with us and discuss the welfare of mankind so that Peace, Unity, and Brotherhood will become part of all men everywhere.

HOPI TRADITIONAL VILLAGE LEADERS, HOPI, 1970

Many religions have been brought to this land. And the way my religion is, they teach me, and they taught me, and told me to respect all religions. And I still do that. And I will until I close

6

my eyes for the last time. When someone else believes what his Creator is, then we can stand and pray together.

HORACE AXTELL, NEZ PERCE, 1992

You, whose day it is, make it beautiful. Get out your rainbow colors, so it will be beautiful.

SONG TO BRING FAIR WEATHER, NOOTKA

Peace ... comes within the souls of men when they realize their relationship, their oneness, with the universe and all its powers, and when they realize that at the center of the Universe dwells Wakan-Tanka, and that this center is really everywhere, it is within each of us.

BLACK ELK, OGLALA LAKOTA, 1947

When this pipe touches your lip, may it operate as a blessing upon all my tribe. May the smoke rise like a cloud, and carry away with it all the animosities which have arisen between us.

BLACK THUNDER, FOX, 1860

The teachings are for all, not just for Indians. ... The white people never wanted to learn before. They thought we were savages. Now they have a different understanding, and they do want to learn. We are all children of God. The tradition is open to anyone who wants to learn. But who really wants to learn?

DON JOSE MATSUWA, HUICHOL, 1989

7

Every part of this soil is sacred in the estimation of my people. Every hillside, every valley, every plain and grove, has been hallowed by some sad or happy event in days long vanished. Even the rocks, which seem to be dumb and dead as they swelter in the sun along the silent shore, thrill with memories of stirring events connected with the lives of my people, and the very dust upon which you now stand responds more lovingly to their footsteps than to yours, because it is rich with the blood of our ancestors and our bare feet are conscious of the sympathetic touch.

CHIEF SEATTLE, DUWAMISH AND SUQUAMISH, 1854

There is one God looking down on us all. We are all children of the one God. God is listening to me. The sun, the darkness, the winds, are all listening to what we now say.

GERONIMO, APACHE, 1886

We do not walk alone. Great Being walks beside us. Know this and be grateful.

POLINGAYSI QÖYAWAYMA, HOPI, 1964

What does it matter how I pray, so long as my prayers are answered?

SITTING BULL, HUNKPAPA LAKOTA, 1887

The white man does not obey the Great Spirit; that is why the Indians never could agree with him.

FLYING HAWK, OGLALA LAKOTA, 1947

8

Oh! No ... I am only going to accept half of your religion. I will belong half to the Christian Religion and half to the Indian, because you may turn out to be wrong after all, and the Indian Religion might happen to be right and then I would have nothing to fall back upon.

PIAPOT (FLASH IN THE SKY), CREE, 1895

Can things go well in a land where freedom of worship is a lie, a hollow boast? To each nation is given the light by which it knows God, and each finds its own way to express the longing to serve Him ... If a nation does not do what is right according to its own understanding, its power is worthless.

THUNDERCHILD, PLAINS CREE, 1973

Brother, if you white men murdered the Son of the Great Spirit, we Indians had nothing to do with it, and it is none of our affair. If he had come among us, we would not have killed him; we would have treated him well. You must make amends for that crime yourselves.

RED JACKET, SENECA, C. 1820

We believed in one God, the Great Spirit. We believed in our own kind of Ten Commandments. And we behaved as though we believed in them.

VINE DELORIA, SR., YANKTON SIOUX, C. 1968

Our religion seems foolish to you, but so does yours to me. The Baptists and Methodists and Presbyterians and the Catholics all have a different God. Why cannot we have one of our own?

SITTING BULL, HUNKPAPA LAKOTA, 1889

◊ ◊ ◊ ◊ ◊

TRADITION, HISTORY

Our people are growing up to realize we mean more to this earth than just a welfare case. We have a history and a language, and nobody else has this particular history and language but us.

EDWARD MOODY, NUXALK (BELLA COOLA), 1986

There is no question that the tribal method of gathering information is more sophisticated and certainly more comprehensive than Western Science. . . . The common knowledge of Indian tribes, when discovered by non-Indian scientists, is seen as an exciting breakthrough. But from the Indian perspective it is mere child's play. It is information which traditional people expected youngsters to acquire as a matter of course.

VINE DELORIA, JR., STANDING ROCK SIOUX, 1992

My children, you have forgotten the customs and traditions of your forefathers. Why do you not clothe yourselves in skins, as they did, use bows and arrows and the stone pointed lances, which they used? You have bought guns, knives, kettles, and blankets from the white man until you can no longer do without them; and what is worse you have drunk the poison firewater, which turns you into fools. Fling all these things away; live as your forefathers did before you.

PONTIAC, ODOWA, 1763

Traditional people of Indian nations have interpreted the two roads that face the light-skinned race as the road to technology and the road to spirituality. We feel that the road to technology ... has led modern society to a damaged and seared earth. Could it be that the road to technology represents a rush to destruction, and that the road to spirituality represents the slower path that the traditional native people have traveled and are now seeking again? The earth is not scorched on this trail. The grass is still growing there.

WILLIAM COMMANDA, MAMIWININI, CANADA, 1991

Times change but principles don't. Times change but lands do not. Times change but our cultures and our languages remain the same. And that's what you have to keep intact. It's not what you wear—it's what's in your heart. And that makes the difference ... Don't forget your home!

OREN LYONS, ONONDAGA, 1992

Experience is the wisest teacher, and history does not furnish an example of a forced civilization being permanent and real.

PLEASANT PORTER, CREEK, 1973

If today I had a young mind to direct, to start on the journey of life, and I was faced with the duty of choosing between the natural way of my forefathers and that of the ... present way of civilization, I would, for its welfare, unhesitatingly set that child's feet in the path of my forefathers. I would raise him to be an Indian!

LUTHER STANDING BEAR, LAKOTA, 1933

We always had plenty; our children never cried from hunger, neither were our people in want ... Our village was healthy and there was no place in the country possessing such advantages, nor hunting grounds better than those we had in possession. If a prophet had come to our village in those days and told us that the things were to take place which have since come to pass, none of our people would have believed him.

BLACK HAWK, SAUK, C. 1830

It is our desire that we and you should be as of one heart, one mind, and one body, thus becoming one people, entertaining a mutual love and regard for each other, to be preserved firm and entire, not only between you and us, but between your children, and our children, to all succeeding generations.

KANICKHUNGO, TRIBE UNKNOWN, 1736

12

Our proud history is unequaled and unsurpassed on this Great Island. Each of us can hold his or her head high, as one of the original people of this beautiful land, and say, "I am an Indian." The Stoney philosophy of living in harmony with nature and in accord with the creations of the Great Spirit will be the theme of many peoples, cultures, and languages who live on this Great Island in the future.

JOHN SNOW, STONEY, 1976

What hurts Indians most is that our costumes are considered beautiful, but it's as if the person wearing them didn't exist.

RIGOBERTA MENCHU, QUICHE MAYA, 1990

I am an old woman now. The buffaloes and black-tail deer are gone, and our Indian ways are almost gone. Sometimes I find it hard to believe that I ever lived them. ... But for me I cannot forget our old ways. ... I seem again to see our Indian village, with smoke curling upward from the earth lodges; and in the river's roar I hear the yells of the warriors, the laughter of little children as of old. ... It is but an old woman's dream. Our Indian life, I know, is gone forever.

BUFFALO BIRD WOMAN, HIDATSA, 1926

You hear talk today about the environment. ... I think this is where they've [dominant society] learned from us. We have been speaking out for so long and have finally been proven correct. It gives one a good feeling. I think, if one sits down and thinks about these things, modern scientific knowledge coupled with the hereditary or traditional knowledge of the people is a powerful instrument for resolving a lot of the difficulties encountered now.

SAUL TERRY, BRIDGE RIVER, VANCOUVER, BC, 1992

Our elders are important, our young people are really important—that's our future. If we can take what our young people have to offer us with their knowledge of today, take the knowledge of our elders with their knowledge of yesterday, and combine those two things, we have something to hand on to our young people's children and their children's children.

ALAN WILSON, HAIDA, BC, 1992

My people were tough in those days ... if in winter a person fell into icy water, he got out, took off his wet clothes, and rolled in the snow, rubbing his body with it, and got warm. Then, after squeezing out the water, he put on his clothes and forgot about getting wet. ... the buffalo-runners rubbed their hands with snow and sand, so that their fingers would be nimble at handling the bow and arrows. Now my people wear gloves, and too many clothes. We are soft as mud.

PRETTY SHIELD, CROW, C. 1925

Once we were happy in our own country and we were seldom hungry, for then the two-leggeds lived together like relatives and there was plenty for them and for us. But the Wasichus came, and they have made little islands for us and other little islands for the four-leggeds, and always these islands are becoming smaller, for around them surges the gnawing flood of the Wasichu; and it is dirty with lies and greed.

BLACK ELK, OGLALA LAKOTA, 1932

14

We have to look at the way we were in the past, hang on to it in our hearts and at the same time change; accept we're always changing to survive.

DOROTHY HABERMAN, YUROK, 1992

◊ ◊ ◊ ◊ ◊

WOMEN AND MEN

Now you have lit a fire and that fire should not go out. The two of you now have a fire that represents love, understanding and a philosophy of life. It will give you heat, food, warmth and happiness. This new fire represents a new beginning—a new life and a new family. The fire should keep burning; you should stay together. You have lit the fire for life, until old age separates you.

WEDDING CEREMONY, NAVAJO, UNDATED

A Sundance woman is like the morning star, filled with spiritual beauty, wisdom, and knowledge. Men and women are the most powerful of the polarities. We walk beside men as equal partners. It takes men and women who have respect and love for one another to live within the embrace of father sky and mother earth. Men and women have an awesome responsibility in maintaining the continuity of this life; the home is the most sacred place in the universe. I walk proudly beside all of you men.

DR. HENRIETTA MANN, SOUTHERN CHEYENNE, 1992

There is a special magic and holiness about the girl and woman. They are the bringers of life to the people, and the teachers of the little children.

SWEET MEDICINE, CHEYENNE, UNDATED

The honor of the people lies in the moccasin tracks of the women. Walk the good road. . . . Be dutiful, respectful, gentle and modest, my daughter. And proud walking. . . . Be strong, with the warm, strong heart of the earth. No people goes down until their women are weak and dishonored, or dead upon the ground. Be strong and sing the strength of the Great Powers within you, all around you.

VILLAGE WISE MAN, SIOUX, 1961

It is well to be good to women in the strength of our man-hood because we must sit under their hands at both ends of our lives.

HE DOG, OGLALA LAKOTA, C. 1900

I want to pay a tremendous respect to the women—our womenfolk. Man may slay one another but cannot ever over-come the woman. For in the quietude of her lap lies the child. You can slay him once and again. But he issues as often from that same gentle lap, a gift to the Great Good in which man is only an accomplice. That's all we are. We're only an accomplice. The woman needs us only for one night. Here we stand in eagle feathers and war bonnets and all that. And our women, so gentle, so sweet, so kind. Yet the race of man goes on because of our women.

PHIL LANE, SR., YANKTON SIOUX, 1992

Love songs are dangerous. If a man gets to singing them we send for a medicine man to treat him and make him stop.

ANONYMOUS TRIBESMAN, TOHONO O'ODHAM, 1926

No indiscretion can banish a woman from her parental lodge—no difference how many children she may bring home, she is always welcome—the kettle is over the fire to feed them.

BLACK HAWK, SAUK, C. 1830

On you [the men] it depends to be a strong help to the women in the raising of children. Share the women's sorrow. Wakan-Tanka smiles on the man who has a kind feeling for a woman.

WHITE BUFFALO CALF WOMAN,
TETON SIOUX, ORAL TRADITION

A great hunter must not be a great lover of women. But no one can help it.

NAJAGNEQ, CIRCUMPOLAR PEOPLES, C. 1927

17

The mainstream culture is not respective of the feminine creative impulse at all. If you go out and look at the images of women—obviously it's become very sick.

LORRAINE CANOE, MOHAWK, 1991

You know, in the old days, it was not so very easy to get a girl when you wanted to be married. Sometimes it was hard work for a young man and he had to stand a great deal.

BLACK ELK, OGLALA LAKOTA, 1932

Men have visions, women have children.

ADELINE WANATEE, MESQUAKIE, 1980

Uncle came home one time and said, "There's something wrong with you. You're not walking right." So I said, "What's the matter with me now?" This was the uncle that gave me all my manhood training. "You need a wife. Then you'll be complete. A wife connects you with the rest of nature; it's supposed to be like that."

JOHN THOMAS, NUU-CHAH-NULTH, C. 1986

See how the boy is with his sister and the other ones of his home lodge and you can know how the man will be with your daughter.

LAKOTA PROVERB

◊ ◊ ◊ ◊ ◊

CHILDREN, EDUCATION

The battle for Indian children will be won in the class-room, not on the streets or on horses. The students of today are our warriors of tomorrow.

EDDIE BOX, SOUTHERN UTE, 1988

I don't think that anybody anywhere can talk about the future of their people or of an organization without talking about education. Whoever controls the education of our children controls our future, the future of the Cherokee people and of the Cherokee Nation, ... We have always placed a great deal of importance on education and that has helped us as a people. We must continue to do that.

WILMA P. MANKILLER, CHEROKEE, 1987

Good acts done for the love of children become stories good for the ears of people from other bands; they become as coveted things, and are placed side by side with the stories of war achievements.

SOCIAL TRADITION, ASSINIBOINE

Training began with children who were taught to sit still and enjoy it. They were taught to use their organs of smell, to look when there was apparently nothing to see, and to listen intently when all seemingly was quiet. A child that cannot sit still is a half-developed child.

LUTHER STANDING BEAR, LAKOTA, 1933

Young children were scolded or lightly punished—the pulling of an ear or switching on the legs—when they disobeyed, falsified, or caused damage in the home. But children above six or seven years of age were expected to know the rules of proper behavior.

PETER SCONCHIN, MODOC, 1963

The hearts of little children are pure, and therefore, the Great Spirit may show to them many things which older people miss.

BLACK ELK, OGLALA LAKOTA, C. 1949

You who are so wise must know that different nations have different conceptions of things; and you will therefore not take it amiss, if our ideas of this kind of education happens not to be the same with yours. We have had some experience of it. Several of our young people were formerly brought up in the Colleges of the Northern Provinces; they were instructed in all your sciences; but, when they came back to us, they were bad runners, ignorant of every means of living in the woods, unable to bear either cold or hunger, knew neither how to build a cabin, take a deer, or kill an enemy, spoke our language imperfectly, were therefore neither fit for hunters, warriors, nor councilors; they were totally good for nothing ...

CANASSATEGO, ONONDAGA, 1744

Civilized people depend too much on man-made printed pages. I turn to the Great Spirit's book which is the whole of his creation. You can read a big part of that book if you study nature. You know, if you take all your books, lay them out under the sun, and let the snow and rain and insects work on them for a while, there will be nothing left. But the Great Spirit has provided you and me an opportunity for study in nature's university—the forests, the rivers, the mountains, and the animals, which include us.

TATANGA MANI (WALKING BUFFALO), STONEY, 1969

Whatever there is for him [an Indian boy] to learn must be learned; whatever qualifications are necessary to a truly great man he must seek at any expense of danger and hardship. Such was the feeling of the imaginative and brave young Indian. It became apparent to him in early life that he must accustom himself to rove alone and not to fear or dislike the impression of solitude.

OHIYESA (DR. CHARLES A. EASTMAN), SANTEE SIOUX, 1902

21

They've always said poor Indians can't speak, so many speak for them. That's why I decided to learn Spanish.

RIGOBERTA MENCHU, QUICHE MAYA, 1990

◊ ◊ ◊ ◊ ◊

ECONOMICS, MONEY AND POWER

Our ancestors were really masters at controlling the environment, simply because they only took what they needed, they did not have to take any more. Now, in the world that we live in, everybody is taking all they can and—I hope I'm wrong—we're headed for a disasterous situation.

NORTON RICKARD, TUSCARORA, 1993

We do not want riches, but we want to train our children right. Riches would do us no good. We could not take them with us to the other world. We do not want riches, we want peace and love.

RED CLOUD, OGLALA LAKOTA, 1870

Indians chase the vision, white men chase the dollar.

JOHN (FIRE) LAME DEER, ROSEBUD LAKOTA, 1972

As Indians we will never have the efficient organization that gains great concessions from society in the marketplace. We will never have a powerful lobby or be a smashing political force. But we will have the intangible unity which has carried us through four centuries of persecution. We are a people unified by our humanity—not a pressure group unified for conquest. And from our greater strength we shall wear down the white man and finally outlast him. We shall endure.

VINE DELORIA, JR., STANDING ROCK SIOUX, 1969

Sometimes I wish the white people hadn't taught us about cash. We had everything, with nature. Now they say we're lazy and give us welfare. But I say, "Who was it that taught us about cash?" It was the white people.

MARGARET SIWALLACE, NUXALK (BELLA COOLA), C. 1986

Our land is more valuable than your money. It will last forever. It will not even perish by the flames of fire. As long as the sun shines and the waters flow this land will be here to give life to men and animals. We cannot sell the lives of men and animals; therefore we cannot sell this land. ...You can count your money and burn it within the nod of a buffalo's head, but only the Great Spirit can count the grains of sand and the blades of grass of these plains. As a present to you, we will give you anything we have that you can take with you; but the land, never.

NORTHERN BLACKFEET CHIEF, 19TH CENTURY

23

Money cannot buy affection.

MANGAS COLORADAS, APACHE, 1851

Look upon the natural resources of this world as capital. No longer look upon them as income. . . . If you look on them as capital then you might find some respect. ... You do not want to lose your capital, because once the capital is gone, of course the income is gone. Our oil, our uranium, our coal, our timber, all of these natural resources are capital. If you look at them as capital, then maybe you will think of the future.

RUSSELL MEANS, LAKOTA, 1977

We can be aggressive and point our finger and be demanding. Quite often this is what society projects us to be. Or we can be cunning and manipulative. The idea of what it takes to be a good businessman and entrepreneur is so opposite to what it takes to be a good human being.

LEONARD GEORGE, BURRARD, BC, 1992

In the absence of the sacred, nothing is sacred—everything is for sale.

OREN LYONS, ONONDAGA, 1992

The white man knows how to make everything, but he does not know how to distribute it.

SITTING BULL, HUNKPAPA LAKOTA, 1885

◊ ◊ ◊ ◊ ◊

LAND, ENVIRONMENT

The signs of the dawn are seen in the east and the breath of the new life is here. Mother earth is the first to be called to awake. She moves, she awakes, she rises, she feels the breath of the new born Dawn. The leaves and the grass stir; all things move with the breath of the new day; Everywhere life is renewed. This is very mysterious; we are speaking of something very sacred, although it happens every day.

THE KURAHUS TAHIRUSSAWICHI, PAWNEE, C. 1900

I don't want to settle. I love to roam over the prairies. There I feel free and happy, but when we settle down we grow pale and die.

SANTANTA, KIOWA, 1867

One does not sell the earth upon which the people walk.

CRAZY HORSE, OGLALA LAKOTA, 1868

For a Western-educated audience the notion of a tree with spirit is a difficult concept to grasp. ... the universe is alive. Therefore, to see a Native speaking with a tree does not carry the message of mental instability; on the contrary, this is a scientist engaged in research!

DR. PAM COLORADO, ONEIDA, 1989

We went to Geneva, the Six Nations [Iroquois], and the great Lakota nation, as representatives of the indigenous people of the Western Hemisphere; and what was the message that we gave? "There is a hue and a cry for human rights," they said, "for all people." And the indigenous people said, "what of the rights of the natural world? Where is the seat for the Buffalo or the Eagle? Who is representing them here in this forum? Who is speaking for the waters of the earth? Who is speaking for the trees and the forests? Who is speaking for the Fish, for the Whales, for the Beavers, for our children?"

OREN LYONS, ONONDAGA, 1990

We are not your slaves. These lakes, these woods and mountains were left us by our ancestors. They are our inheritance; and we will part with them to none. Your nation supposes that we, like the white people, cannot live without bread and pork and beer. But you ought to know that He, the Great Spirit and Master of Life, has provided food for us in these spacious lakes, and on these woody mountains.

PONTIAC, ODAWA, 1762

26

Wars are fought to see who owns the land, but in the end it possesses man. Who dares say he owns it—is he not buried beneath it?

NINO COCHISE, CHIRICAHUA APACHE, 1971

At night when the streets of your cities and villages are silent and you think them deserted, they will throng with the returning hosts that once filled them and still love this beautiful land. The white man will never be alone. Let him be just and deal kindly with my people, for the dead are not powerless. Dead, did I say? There is no death, only a change of worlds.

CHIEF SEATTLE, DUWAMISH AND SQUAMISH, 1854

We're sitting on our blessed Mother Earth from which we get our strength and determination, love and humility—all the beautiful attributes that we've been given. So turn to one another; love one another; respect one another; respect Mother Earth; respect the waters—because that's life itself!

PHIL LANE , SR., YANKTON SIOUX, 1992

The white man saves the whooping crane, he saves the goose in Hawaii, but he is not saving the way of life of the Indian.

ANONYMOUS, BLACKFOOT, C. 1968

No real progress can be made in environmental law unless some of the insights into the sacredness of land derived from traditional tribal religions become basic attitudes of the larger society.

VINE DELORIA, JR., STANDING ROCK SIOUX, 1991

When we Indians kill meat, we eat it all up. When we dig roots, we make little holes. When we built houses, we make little holes. When we burn grass for grasshoppers, we don't ruin things. We shake down acorns and pine nuts. We don't chop down the trees. We only use dead wood. But the white people plow up the ground, pull down the trees, kill everything. ... the White people pay no attention. ... How can

27

the spirit of the earth like the White man? ... everywhere the White man has touched it, it is sore.

WINTU WOMAN, 19TH CENTURY

There is no climate or soil which, to my mind, is equal to that of Arizona. ... It is my land, my home, my father's land, to which I now ask to be allowed to return. I want to spend my last days there, and be buried among those mountains. If this could be, I might die in peace, feeling that my people, placed in their native homes, would increase in numbers, rather than diminish as at present, and that our name would not become extinct. ... I hope that the remnant of the Apache tribe may, when I am gone, be granted the one privilege which they request—to return to Arizona.

GERONIMO, APACHE, 1877

The earth and myself are of one mind. The measure of the land and the measure of our bodies are the same. ... Do not misunderstand me, but understand me fully with reference to my affection to the land. I never said the land was mine to do with it as I chose. The one who has the right to dispose of it is the one who created it. I claim a right to live on my land, and accord you the privilege to live on yours.

CHIEF JOSEPH, NEZ PERCE, C. 1875

We know our lands have now become more valuable: the white people think we do not know their value; but we are sensible that the land is everlasting, and the few goods we receive for it are soon worn out and gone ...

CANASSATEGO, ONONDAGA, 1742

In recent years we have come to understand what progress is. It is the total replacement of nature by an artificial tech-

28

nology. Progress is the absolute destruction of the real world
in favor of a technology that creates a comfortable way of
life for a few fortunately situated people. Within our lifetime
the difference between the Indian use of land and the white
use of land will become crystal clear. The Indian lived with
his land. The white destroyed his land. He destroyed the
planet earth.

VINE DELORIA, JR., STANDING ROCK SIOUX, 1970

The hybrid corn has no taste, and when my neighbors save
its seeds to regrow the following year, only small, irregular
ears are produced. That is why I save the native seed, but the
other people don't anymore. ... Let me predict something: If
they don't start protecting the native seeds around here, local
food production will eventually decline. The quality of the
annual crops and even of the fruit trees will fail if we become
dependent upon introduced hybrids.

CASIMIRO SANCHEZ, SONORAN, 1992

If I go to Panama City and stand in front of a pharmacy, and,
because I need medicine, pick up a rock and break the window,
you would take me away and put me in jail. For me, the forest is
my pharmacy. If I have sores on my legs, I go to the forest and
get the medicine I need to cure them. The forest is also a great
refrigerator. It keeps the food I need fresh. If I need a peccary, I
go to the forest with my rifle and—pow!—take out food for
myself and my family. But we can take what we need without
having to destroy everything as your people do.

RAFAEL HARRIS, KUNA, TO OMAR TORRIJOS, 1980

29

I remember watching my father cut down a cedar tree from
which he was going to make a large dugout canoe. He car-

ried out his work with great respect for the tree. He would talk to it as though to a fellow human being. He would ask the tree not to hurt him, as he was going to change it into a beautiful object that would be useful to him.

PETER WEBSTER, AHOUSAHT, 1983

We told them that the supernatural powers, Taku Wakan, had given the Lakota the buffalo for food and clothing. We told them that where the buffalo ranged, that was our country. We told them that the buffalo must have their country and the Lakota must have the buffalo.

RED CLOUD, OGLALA LAKOTA, 1903

I love the land and the buffalo and will not part with it. I want you to understand well what I say.

SANTANTA, KIOWA, 1867

Corn is a metaphor for how we look at nature and how we use science for the betterment of human beings and the planet.

KATSI COOK, MOHAWK, 1992

We didn't own the land. We were caretakers. I'd say we owned the path that we walked.

CURLEY BEAR WAGNER, BLACKFEET, 1993

◊ ◊ ◊ ◊ ◊

INSIGHT, APPRECIATION

We may *misunderstand*, but we do not *misexperience*.
VINE DELORIA, JR. , STANDING ROCK SIOUX, 1991

It's OK to do nothing. We are compelled in the Western culture to have a plan, to execute, to move on some orderly schedule. That's baloney! It's OK to do nothing. Sometimes you'll infuriate your Western counterpart. They'll think you don't care or that you have a secret. The reality is you do have a secret.
GENE KELUCHE, WINTU, 1992

The frog does not drink up the pond in which he lives.
ORAL TRADITION, TETON SIOUX

Argument doesn't pay: you don't come home happy.

ORAL TRADITION, HOPI

Those who know how to play can easily leap over the adversaries of life. And one who knows how to sing and laugh never brews mischief.

PROVERB, IGLULIK

Today we are blessed with this beautiful baby. May his feet be to the east; his right hand to the south; his head to the west; his left hand to the north. May he walk and dwell on Mother Earth peacefully.

TOM RATION, CHILD BLESSING PRAYER, NAVAJO, 1975

The great sea has sent me adrift. It moves me as the weed in a great river. Earth and the great weather move me, have carried me away, and move my inward parts with joy.

UVAVNUK, IGLULIK, C. 1920

The sky blesses me; the earth blesses me. Up in the skies I cause the spirits to dance. On the earth, the people I cause to dance.

CREE ROUND DANCE SONG, SPOKEN BY FINE DAY, 1941

At the edge of the mountain, a cloud hangs. And there my heart, my heart, my heart, hangs with it. At the edge of the mountain, a cloud trembles. And there my heart, my heart, my heart, trembles with it.

RAIN SONG, TOHONO O'ODHAM, UNDATED

It was the wind that gave them life. It is the wind that comes out of our mouths now that gives us life. When this ceases to blow we die. In the skin at the tips of our fingers we see the trail of the wind; it shows us where the wind blew when our ancestors were created.

IT WAS THE WIND, NAVAJO, 19TH CENTURY

We are related, we are all one. The Indian acknowledges this and so discovers the most liberating aspect of Native science: *life renews*, and all things which support life are renewable.

DR. PAM COLORADO, ONEIDA, 1989

The Eskimo asked the local missionary priest, "If I did not know about God and sin, would I go to Hell?" "No," said the priest, "not if you did not know." "Then why, "asked the Eskimo earnestly, "did you tell me?"

CIRCUMPOLAR PEOPLE'S STORY, UNDATED

Crisis changes people and turns ordinary people into wiser or more responsible ones.

WILMA P. MANKILLER, CHEROKEE, 1987

Now I know the government is going to break the Treaty because when it was signed it was understood that it would last as long as the grass grew, the winds blew, the rivers ran, and men walked on two legs—and now they have sent us an Agent who has only one leg.

PIAPOT (FLASH IN THE SKY), CREE, 1895

Sometimes dreams are wiser than waking.

BLACK ELK, OGLALA LAKOTA, 1931

The smarter a man is the more he needs God to protect him from thinking he knows everything.

GEORGE WEBB, PIMA, 1959

Those who essay to walk the medicine path hoping for a more pleasurable existence are bound to be disappointed. Each increment of power one gains along the path of power requires sacrifice and exacts its toll of suffering and pain. In the universe of power everything has its price.

PAULA GUNN ALLEN, LAGUNA, 1991

Agreements the Indian makes with the government are like the agreement a buffalo makes with the hunter after it has been pierced by many arrows. All it can do is lie down and give in.

CHIEF OURAY, UTE, C . 1868

We move forward and become like that which we think about. Isn't it time we began to think about what we're thinking about?

DON COYHIS, MOHICAN, 1993

Provocations of emotion are much superior to provocations of the mind alone.

VINE DELORIA, JR., STANDING ROCK SIOUX, 1991

And that, I guess, is what it all boils down to—do the right thing, everything goes fine; do the wrong thing, everything's a mess.

ROBERT SPOTT, YUROK, 1890

34

◇ ◇ ◇ ◇ ◇

PHILOSOPHY, CULTURE

Let me be a free man—free to travel, free to stop, free to work, free to trade where I choose, free to choose my own teachers, free to follow the religion of my fathers, free to think and talk and act for myself—and I will obey every law, or submit to the penalty.

CHIEF JOSEPH, NEZ PERCE, 1877

Choose those pursuits which give you the greatest joy; you will do them much better. Do not let somebody prescribe for you what should be your life. Wait and see; weigh and feel the flow. Then you will be fulfilled, and you will perform much better.

GENE KELUCHE, WINTU, 1992

Much has been said of the want of what you term "Civilization" among the Indians. Many proposals have been made to us to adopt your laws, your religion, your manners, and your customs. We do not see the propriety of such a reformation. We should be better pleased with beholding the good effects of these doctrines in your own practices than with hearing you talk about them, or of reading your newspapers on such subjects.

OLD TASSEL, CHEROKEE, 1777

When your time comes to die, be not like those whose hearts are filled with the fear of death, so when their time comes they weep and pray for a little more time to live their lives over again in a different way. Sing your death song, and die like a hero going home.

TECUMSEH, SHAWNEE, C. 1800

Why do you believe letters and arts superior to the pursuits of the bow and arrow? Do they more truly fulfill the ambitions of the human heart, according to the measure of light and knowledge, which determine the actual conditions of the different races of men?

CHIEF AUPAUMUT, MOHICAN, C. 1725

I do not think Congress is going to pass a law terminating the Omaha Tribe. I think the Bureau of Indian Affairs is going to terminate the tribe by taking away the Agency services and selling our Omaha lands. I say, most humbly, to the respected officials, that cheaper administration, even better administration, is not everything. The good and happiness of the people is everything ...

ALFRED W. GILPIN, OMAHA, 1954

36

You take something of yourself and give it free of charge. You take a part of yourself and do so because you believe you are connected to everything else. You become aware of yourself as a part of everything. You suffer momentarily so that someone else will not have to.

UNKNOWN, WINNEBAGO, BEFORE 1945

Too much thought only leads to trouble. We Eskimos do not concern ourselves with solving all the riddles. We repeat the old stories in the way they were told to us, and with the words we ourselves remember. And if there should then seem to be a lack of reason in the story as a whole, there is yet enough remaining in the way of incomprehensible happenings, which our thought cannot grasp.

ORULO, IGLULIK, C. 1930

I have advised my people thus: when you find anything good in the white man's road, pick it up; but when you find something bad, or that turns out bad, drop it, leave it alone.

SITTING BULL, HUNKPAPA LAKOTA, 1887

The man who sat on the ground in his tipi meditating on life and its meaning, accepting the kinship of all creatures and acknowledging unity with the universe of things was infusing into his being the true essence of civilization. And when native man left off this form of development, his humanization was retarded in growth.

LUTHER STANDING BEAR, LAKOTA, 1933

37

We want none of your laws or customs that we have not willingly adopted for ourselves. We have adopted many. You have adopted some of ours—votes for women for instance—

We are as well behaved as you and you would think so if you knew us better.

EDWARD AHENAKEW, CREE, 1920

He [uncle] would always say to me, "You ought to follow the example of the shunktokecha [wolf]. Even when he is surprised and runs for his life, he will pause to take one more look at you before he enters his final retreat. So you must take a second look at everything you see."

OHIYESA (DR. CHARLES A. EASTMAN), SANTEE SIOUX, 1902

White men have education and books, and ought to know exactly what to do, but hardly any two of them agree on what should be done.

SPOTTED TAIL, SICANGU LAKOTA, C. 1880

We are told by some thinkers that between the material and the spiritual parts of man there is a great division, that there is no shading of one into the other. I cannot believe that. One affects the other, and the place where a man lives can shape his character.

OLD KEYAM, PLAINS CREE, 1973

Every life is a circle. And within every life are smaller circles. A part of our lives goes full circle every seven years. We speak of living in cycles of seven.

BARBARA MEANS ADAMS, LAKOTA, 1990

38

◊ ◊ ◊ ◊ ◊

LEADERSHIP

The leadership systems currently in place too often look at us as our *doing*, and they say *do* differently in order to change. But the Indian way says we're not human *doings*, we're human beings. If we want to change the *doing* in leadership, I need to change my being. And the way to change my being is to change my intent.

DON COYHIS, MOHICAN, 1993

We do now crown you with the sacred emblem of the antlers, the sign of your lordship. You shall now become a mentor of the people of the Five Nations. The thickness of your skin will be seven spans, for you will be proof against anger, offensive action and criticism. With endless patience you shall carry out your duty, and your firmness shall be tempered with calm deliberation. In all your official acts, self-interest shall be cast aside. You shall look and listen to the welfare of the whole people, and have always in view, not only the present but the coming generations—the unborn of the future Nation.

THE PEACE MAKER, IROQUOIS ORAL TRADITION

The issue of Native people's survival is dependent on the notion of cooperating more than leading people. Working with people, once we all realized that there really wasn't any leadership per se, the problems with leadership went away. It wasn't such a big issue any more. ... leadership is really not the issue at all. Everybody has to play a part and we have to go ahead and do what we have to do.

AGNES WILLIAMS, SENECA, 1992

The plains are large and wide. We are the children of the plains, it is our home, and the Buffalo has been our food always. I hope you look upon the Blackfeet, Bloods, and Sarcees as your children now, and that you will be indulgent and charitable to them. ... The advice given me and my people has proved to be very good. If the Police had not come to the country, where would we be all now? Bad men and whiskey were killing us so fast that very few, indeed, of us would have been left today. The Police have protected us as the feathers of the bird protect it from the frosts of winter. I wish them all good, and trust that all our hearts will increase in goodness from this time forward. I am satisfied. I will sign the treaty.

CROWFOOT, BLACKFOOT, 1877

40

Self-government means you want to be the boss over what happens to the people on a day-to-day basis and what happens to the people in the future. We have to be able to make decisions to protect our people, the lands, the water, the air and so on. ... Self-government is establishing something that we can safeguard for the future. It's your traditional way that you carry on your day-to-day, year-to-year business, from generation to generation.

SAUL TERRY, BRIDGE RIVER, BC, 1992

As the [Indigenous] culture is taking hold again among the tribes all along the Northwest Coast, people are beginning to realize the value of our elders, of our hereditary chiefs, and what has to be done in our villages. ... In our Haida Nation what they want to do is get hold of our hereditary chiefs and start ... using them like they've done before. ... I think things are going to start to change in the near future concerning our hereditary chiefs. They're going to have a lot more to say in a lot of things, instead of being symbolic heads, as the white society sees us. Instead of just being symbolic heads, we should have a real solid part in everything.

ALAN WILSON, HAIDA, BC, 1992

The knowledge of the whereabouts [of the Sacred Tree], and of the fruits that adorn its branches have always been carefully guarded and preserved within the minds and hearts of our wise elders and leaders. These humble, loving and dedicated souls will guide anyone who is honestly and sincerely seeking along the path leading to the protecting shadow of the Sacred Tree.

FOUR WORLDS DEVELOPMENT PROJECT, 1984

41

Show respect for all men, but grovel to none.

TECUMSEH, SHAWNEE, C. 1800

A man was chief only as long as he did the will of the people. If he got to be too chiefy, he'd go to sleep one night, and wake up the next morning to find that he was chief all to himself. The tribe would move away in the night, and they didn't wait four years to do it either.

SUN BEAR, CHIPPEWA, 1970

I am not only your chief but an old man, and your father. It therefore becomes my duty to advise you. I know how hard it is for youth to listen to the voice of age. The old blood creeps with the snail, but the young blood leaps with the torrent. Once I was young, my sons, and thought as you do now. Then my people were strong and my voice was ever for war. ... You must not fight the whites; and I not only advise against it, I forbid it.

WASHAKIE, SHOSHONE, 1870

A man should rely on his own resources; the one who so trains himself is ready for any emergency.

ORAL TRADITION, OMAHA

Oh God! Like the Thunderbird of old I shall grab the instruments of the white man's success—his education, his skills—and with these new tools I shall build my race into the proudest segment of your society. ... I shall see our young braves and our chiefs sitting in the houses of law and government, ruling and being ruled by the knowledge and freedom of our great land. So shall we shatter the barriers of our isolation.

DAN GEORGE, COAST SALISH, 1967

The path to glory is rough, and many gloomy hours obscure it.

BLACK HAWK, SAUK, 1833

42

STRUGGLE, CONFLICT, TREATIES

To the Indians of Canada, the treaties represent an Indian Magna Carta. The treaties are important to us because we entered into those negotiations with faith, with hope for a better life with honor. We have survived for over a century with little but that hope. Did the white man enter into them with something less in mind?

HAROLD CARDINAL, CREE, 1969

Every struggle, whether won or lost, strengthens us for the next to come. It is not good for people to have an easy life. They become weak and inefficient when they cease to struggle. Some need a series of defeats before developing the strength and courage to win a victory.

VICTORIO, MIMBRES APACHE, 1970

They could not capture me except under a white flag. They cannot hold me except with a chain.

OSCEOLA, SEMINOLE, 1838

What treaty that the whites have kept has the Red Man broken? Not one. What treaty that the white man ever made with us have they kept? Not one. When I was a boy the Sioux owned the world; the sun rose and set on their land; they sent ten thousand men to battle. Where are the warriors today? Who slew them? Where are our lands? Who owns them? What white man can ever say I ever stole his land or a penny of his money? Yet, they say I am a thief. What white woman, however lonely, was ever captive or insulted by me? Yet they saw I am a bad Indian. What white man has ever seen me drunk? Who has ever come to me hungry or unfed? Who has ever seen me beat my wives or abuse my children? What law have I broken? Is it wrong for me to love my own? Is it wicked for me because my skin is red? Because I am a Sioux; because I was born where my father lived; because I would die for my people and my country?

SITTING BULL, HUNKPAPA LAKOTA, 1885

44

That people will continue longest in the enjoyment of peace who timely prepare to vindicate themselves and manifest a determination to protect themselves whenever they are wronged.

TECUMSEH, SHAWNEE, C. 1800

Fair is the clear sky, and green grass, yet more fair is peace among men.

WAWAN CEREMONY, OMAHA

I am Dekanawidah, and with the Five Nations confederate I plant the Tree of the Great Peace. ... I name the ree the Tree of the Great Long Leaves. Under the shade of this Tree of the Great Peace we spread the soft white feather down of the globe thistle as seats for you, Atotarho and your cousin lords. Roots have spread out from the Tree, and the name of these roots is the Great White Roots of Peace. If any man of any nation shall show a desire to obey the laws of the Great Peace, they shall trace the roots to their source, and they shall be welcomed to take shelter beneath the Tree of the Long Leaves. The smoke of the confederate council fire shall pierce the sky so that all nations may discover the central council fire of the Great Peace. I, Dekanawidah, and the confederate lords now uproot the tallest pine tree and into the cavity thereby made we cast all weapons of war. Into the depth of the earth, down into the deep under earth currents of water flowing into unknown regions, we cast all weapons of war. We bury them from sight forever and plant again the Tree.

THE PEACE MAKER, IROQUOIS ORAL TRADITION, C. 1000

Hear me my chiefs! I am tired; my heart is sick and sad. From where the sun now stands I will fight no more forever.

CHIEF JOSEPH, NEZ PERCE, 1877

45

We preferred our own way of living. We were no expense to the government. All we wanted was peace and to be left alone.

CRAZY HORSE, OGLALA LAKOTA, 1877

You cannot change my color. You cannot change the color of my eyes. Neither can you change my hair. I am born a Native American Indian and I will die an Indian. ... we have resisted the system and we have proved our existence and we have come here to let you know that we still exist as human beings.

PHILLIP DEERE, MUSKOGEE-CREEK, 1977

Why will you take by force what you may obtain by love? Why will you destroy us who supply you with food? What can you get by war? ... We are unarmed, and willing to give you what you ask, if you come in a friendly manner ...

I am not so simple as not to know it is better to eat good meat, sleep comfortably, live quietly with my women and children, laugh and be merry with the English, and being their friend, trade for their copper and hatchets, than to run away from them. ... Take away your guns and swords, the cause of all our jealousy, or you may die in the same manner.

POWHATAN, ALGONQUIN, 1609

There is only one color of mankind that is not allowed to participate in the international community. And that color is red.

RUSSELL MEANS, LAKOTA, 1977

Christopher Columbus is a symbol, not of a man, but of imperialism. ... Imperialism and colonialism are not something that happened decades ago or generations ago, but they are still happening now with the exploitation of people. ... The kind of thing that took place long ago in which people were dispossessed from their land and forced out of subsistence economies and into market economies—those processes are still happening today.

JOHN MOHAWK, SENECA, 1992

JUSTICE, RECONCILIATION, PEACE

We, who are clay blended by the Master Potter, come from the kiln of Creation in many hues. How can people say one skin is colored, when each has its own coloration? What should it matter that one bowl is dark and the other pale, if each is of good design and serves its purpose well?

POLINGAYSI QÖYAWAYMA, HOPI, 1964

We need to put our tomahawks away. We need to work together as a community of scholars, of engineers and of scientists. ... We need to survive the pressures of all the things that are happening in this country. For the survival of the Native American we need community. We need to work to-

gether. We need to put down our differences and work together for the benefit of our people and our elders ...

DR. FRED BEGAY, NAVAJO, 1992

Treat all men alike. Give them all the same law. Give them all
an even chance to live and grow. All men were made by the
same Great Spirit Chief. They are all brothers. The earth is the
mother of all people, and all people shall have equal rights upon
it. You might as well expect the rivers to run backward as that
any man who was born a free man should be contented penned
up and denied liberty to go where he pleases.

CHIEF JOSEPH, NEZ PERCE, 1879

The lesson which seems so hard to learn is that of dignity
and respect. ... [Native voices complain about] the continu-
ing propensity of the white man to change the terms of the
debate to favor himself. But deep down these are cries about
dignity, complaints about the lack of respect. "It is not necessary," Sitting Bull said, "that eagles should be crows."

VINE DELORIA, JR. , STANDING ROCK SIOUX, 1991

No man should seek to destroy the special genius that race
ancestry gives him. The God of nations did not give races
distinctive racial endowments and characteristics for naught.
And now with a coming race consciousness the American
Indian seeks to go even further and say, "I am not a red man
only, I am an American in the truest sense, and a brother man
to all humankind."

ARTHUR C. PARKER, SENECA, 1916

A great many years ago the government commenced feeding
us and clothing us. Do they want to keep it up until our children's
children and their children's children are old men and women?

48

No, we don't want it so. We think we have been given enough, meaning rations and clothing. We want to be free now.

ASA DAKLUGIE, NEDNHI APACHE, 1909

In our language there is no word to say inferior or superiority or equality because we are equal, it's a known fact. But life has become very complicated since the newcomers came here. And how does your spirit react to it? ... It's painful. You have to be strong to walk through the storm. I know I'm a bridge between two worlds. All I ask is for people to wash their feet before they try to walk on me.

ALANIS OBOMSAWIN, ABENAKI, 1982

We want to change the image that has been portrayed by John Wayne, the media, and the history books. We want to portray the truth. We, the Indian people, the Red Man of the Western Hemisphere, are the truth of the Western Hemisphere!

CLYDE BELLECOURT, OJIBWAY, 1978

No longer should the Indian be dehumanized in order to make material for lurid and cheap fiction to embellish street-stands. Rather, a fair and correct history of the Native American should be incorporated in the curriculum of the public school.

LUTHER STANDING BEAR, LAKOTA, 1933

The view of Indians as hostile savages who capture white ladies and torture them, obstruct the westward movement of peaceable white settlers, and engage in bloodthirsty uprisings in which they glory in the massacre of innocent colonists and pioneers, is dear to the hearts of producers of bad films and even worse television. However, it is this view that is most deeply embedded in the American unconscious, where it forms the basis for much of the social oppression of other people of color and of women.

PAULA GUNN ALLEN, LAGUNA, 1991

49

COMMUNITY

If you have one hundred people who live together, and if each one cares for the rest, there is One Mind.

SHINING ARROWS, CROW, 1972

Hear me! A single twig breaks, but the bundle of twigs is strong.

TECUMSEH, SHAWNEE, 1795

The old people said, "Have patience, young man. Look around you. Understand who you are, where you come from, and why and where you are going. Understand that time is on your side and just because someone has invented a clock does not mean you have to hurry through life. Clocks are for those who are going to be trained to do the bidding of the master. Time is on your side. If you understand that you'll know how to utilize time. Therefore life is no longer a problem. Today is no longer a problem. Your teenage years are no longer a problem. Nothing is a problem because you understand that there is no time."

RUSSELL MEANS, LAKOTA, 1988

The tipi encloses a circular space that has no end ... whereas the log cabin formed a square with exact dimensions marking the ends of the walls. The design of this log cabin reflects the non-Indians' way of life, exemplified by a need to find exact distances, time increments, philosophical definitions, and finite answers to scientific riddles in a materialistic world filled with the implements of technology. The tipi is the Plains Indians' contribution to the architecture of the Americas. The tipi taught the tribal members to recycle a space for many uses, and the communal space of the tipi helped develop the tribe's interpersonal relationship norms.

DENNIS SUN RHODES, ARAPAHOE, 1993

The elders say, "The longest road you're going to have to walk in your life is from from here to here. From the head to the heart." But they also say you can't speak to the people as a leader unless you've made the return journey. From the heart back to the head.

PHIL LANE, JR., YANKTON SIOUX, 1992

I live in fear! There is no man I hate, no matter who he is, or what he is. But I live in fear of the white man. I fear the death he possesses. I fear the violence that is in him. And I would not be surprised if one day the white man killed himself, and all of us. I live in terrible fear of that.

The white man hates himself. And he hates the Great Spirit. I think of that sometimes. Why else would the white man do the things he does? The things he has done to the Indians? To everyone? I do not believe that the white man feels guilty, as they say; he is too full of hate.

VINE DELORIA, SR., YANKTON SIOUX, 1968

SOURCES

The following publishers have generously given permission to use quotations from copyrighted works.

Akwe:kon Journal, Fall 1992, Spring 1993.

American Indian Ecology, J. Donald Hughes, 1983, Texas Western Press.

American Indian Women Telling Their Lives, Gretchen M. Bataille and Kathleen Mullen Sands, 1987, University of Nebraska Press.

Bury My Heart at Wounded Knee, Dee Brown, Bantam Edition 1972, Bantam Books, Holt, Rinehart and Winston.

Chief Joseph's Own Story, 1984, Ye Galleon Press.

Circle Without End, Frances G. and Gerald Scott Lombardi, 1983, Naturegraph Publishers, Inc.

Cry of the Thunderbird, Charles Hamilton, 1972, University of Oklahoma Press.

First People, First Voices, Penny Petrone, Editor, 1983, University of Toronto Press.

Grandmothers of the Light, Paula Gunn Allen, 1991, Beacon Press.

I Have Spoken: American History Through the Voices of the Indians, Virginia Armstrong, 1984, Swallow Press Books, Ohio University Press.

I, Rigoberta Menchu, Elisabeth Burgos-Debray, Editor, 1993, Verso.

Indian Country, Peter Matthiessen, 1984, Penguin Books.

Indian Oratory, W. C. Vanderwerth, 1971, University of Oklahoma Press.

Indian Roots of American Democracy, José Barreiro, Editor, 1992, Akwe:kon Press.

Lame Deer Seeker of Visions, John (Fire) Lame Deer and Richard Erdoes, 1976, Washington Square Press.

My Indian Boyhood, Luther Standing Bear, 1931, 1988, University of Nebraska Press.

Native American Reader, Jerry D. Blanche, Ph.D., Editor, 1990, The Denali Press.

Native American Testimony, Peter Nabakov, Editor, 1991, Viking Penguin.

Native Peoples, Media Concepts Group, Inc., for The National Museum of the American Indian of The Smithsonian Institution and eight regional museums, winter 1991, spring 1993.

New Voices From the Longhouse, Joseph Bruchac, Editor, 1989, The Greenfield Review Press.

Our Chiefs and Elders, David Neal, 1992, University of Washington Press.

Our Voices, Our Vision: American Indians Speak on Quality in Education, (AISES) for the College Entrance Examination Board, 1989.

Parabola Magazine, winter, VI: 1.

People of the Shining Mountains, Charles S. Marsh, 1982, Pruett Publishing Co.

Prayers of Smoke: Renewing Makah Tribal Tradition, Barbara Means Adams, 1990, Celestial Arts.

Profiles in Wisdom, Steven McFadden, 1991, Bear & Co., Inc.

Sitting Bull: Champion of the Sioux, Stanley Vestal, 1932, 1989, University of Oklahoma Press.

The Sacred, Peggy V. Beck and A. L. Waters, 1977, Navajo Community College Press.

The Sacred Tree, The Four Worlds Development Project, 1984, Four Worlds Development Press (Canada) and Lotus Light Publications.

Touch the Earth: A Self-Portrait of Indian Existence, T. C. McLuhan, 1971, Touchstone Books, Simon & Schuster.

Turtle Quarterly, spring and summer 1992.

Winds of Change, winter 1992, autumn 1992, spring 1993, summer 1993, winter 1994, AISES Publishing, Inc.

Women in Navajo Society, Ruth Roessel, 1981, Navajo Resource Center.

Unpublished speeches presented at AISES Leadership Conferences, the State of the Indian Nation Conference and the Association on American Indian Affairs.

INDEX OF SPEAKERS

Barbara Means Adams, 38
Edward Ahenakew, 37–38
Paula Gunn Allen, 34, 49
Assiniboine Social Tradition, 20
Chief Aupaumut, 36
Horace Axtell, 6–7
Dr. Eunice Baumann-Nelson, 3
Dr. Fred Begay, 47–48
Clyde Bellecourt, 49
Black Elk, xi, 7, 14, 18, 20, 33
Black Hawk, 12, 17, 42
Black Thunder, 7
Eddie Box, 19
Buffalo Bird Woman, 13
Dr. Gregory Cajete, 3
Canassatego, 20–21, 28
Lorraine Canoe, 17
Harold Cardinal, 43
Nino Cochise, 26
Mangas Coloradas, 23
Dr. Pam Colorado, 26, 33
William Commanda, 11
Katsi Cook, 30
Don Coyhis, 34, 39
Crazy Horse, 26, 45
Cree Round Dance Song, 32
Crowfoot, 40
Asa Daklugie, 48–49
Phillip Deere, 46
Vine Deloria, Jr., 10–11, 23, 27,
    28–29, 31, 34, 48
Vine Deloria, Sr., 9, 51–52

Flying Hawk, 8
Four Worlds Development
    Project, 41
Dan George, 42
Leonard George, 24
Geronimo, 8, 28
Alfred W. Gilpin, 36
Dorothy Haberman, 14
Rafael Harris, 29
He Dog, 16
Hopi Oral Tradition, 32
Hopi Traditional Village
    Leaders, 6
Iglulik Proverb, 32
It Was The Wind, 33
Chief Joseph, 28, 35, 45, 48
Kanickhungo, 12
Karoniaktatie (Alex Jacobs), 2
Gene Keluche, 2, 31, 35
Kurahus Tahirussawichi, The, 25
Lakota Proverb, 18
John (Fire) Lame Deer, 2, 3, 23
Phil Lane, Jr., 51
Phil Lane, Sr., 16–17, 27
Oren Lyons, 5–6, 11, 24, 26
Wilma P. Mankiller, 19, 33
Dr. Henrietta Mann, 15–16
Don Jose Matsuwa, 7
Russell Means, 24, 46, 50–51
Rigoberta Menchu, 13, 21
John Mohawk, 46
N. Scott Momaday, 1

Edward Moody, 10
Najagneq, 17
Navajo Wedding Ceremony, 15
Nootka Song to Bring Fair
    Weather, 7
Alanis Obomsawin, 49
Ohiyesa (Dr. Charles A.
    Eastman), 4, 6, 21, 38
Old Keyam, 38
Old Tassel, 36
Omaha Oral Tradition, 42
Omaha Wawan Ceremony, 45
Orulo, 37
Osceola, 44
Chief Ouray, 34
Arthur C. Parker, 48
Peace Maker, 39–40, 45
Piapot (Flash in the Sky), 8, 33
Pontiac, 11, 26
Pleasant Porter, 12
Tom Porter, 6
Powhatan, 46
Pretty Shield, 14
Al Qöyawayma, 4
Polingaysi Qöyawayma, 2, 8, 47
Tom Ration, 32
Red Cloud, 22, 30
Red Jacket, 9
Dennis Sun Rhodes, 51
Norton Rickard, 22
Casimiro Sanchez, 29
Santanta, 25, 30
Peter Sconchin, 20
Chief Seattle, 7–8, 27

Shining Arrows, 50
Sitting Bull, 8, 9, 24, 37, 44
Margaret Siwallace, 23
John Snow, 12–13
Robert Spott, 34
Spotted Tail, 38
Luther Standing Bear, 12, 20, 37,
    49
Sun Bear, 42
Sweet Medicine, 16
Tachnechdorus (Logan), 3
Don Talayesva, 2
Tatanga Mani (Walking Buffalo),
    4, 21
Tecumseh, 2, 36, 41, 44, 50
Saul Terry, 13, 41
Teton Sioux Oral Tradition, 31
John Thomas, 18
Thunderchild, 9
Tohono O'odham Oral
    Tradition, 32
Turtleheart, 6
Uvavnuk, 32
Victorio, 43–44
Curly Bear Wagner, 30
Adeline Wanatee, 18
Washakie, 42
George Webb, 33
Peter Webster, 29–30
White Buffalo Calf Woman, 17
Agnes Williams, 40
Alan Wilson, 13–14, 41
Wintu Woman, 27–28